781950 433261

My Dear one
JLt

Boardwalk Dreams

Boardwalk Dreams

poems by
Dominic Albanese

Poetic Justice Books
Port St. Lucie, Florida

Published by Poetic Justice Books
Port Saint Lucie, Florida
www.poeticjusticebooks.com

ISBN: 978-1-950433-26-1

FIRST EDITION [thus]
10 9 8 7 6 5 4 3 2 1

contents

Boardwalk Dreams

subway train
track noise
fills the tunnel
the D train
to Coney Island

the ghost of my father
is riding the seat behind me
there is no one else
in the car

then
the door opens
I leave
he stays
seagulls fly overhead

Love

whenever he asked her
a question
with his eyes
she was unable
to answer
every emotion between
them was another reminder
of what
they meant
yet
did not
mean to
each other

Musing

selected history
        certain poems
            a look
                some women's look
        in passing
the way light
runs up
Mission Street
or bounces off Noe Valley

        the arboretum
            ocean beach
everywhere
        no place special
as you see
as you are
one idea is as good
as another

True or False

I think
I am afraid of women
this is a revelation
of late
now I write a lot about them
their scent, their looks, their mystery
mostly their mystery
what is unknown is usually feared

it is what I do not know
how can I claim to love them
and not know them
not individually but amass
women's laughter haunts my dreams
not at me, just in passing

they know things I don't
how the world really is
not some poetic mist-filled hopefulness
taking into account the abuse they suffer
in other parts of the world
free women seem to counteract it by
deep secret sisterhood ritual

ok, this is something
I need to work on, along
with my other maladies
can't even fix cars right these days
how in hell
am I supposed to figure out the biggest
most complicated issue of my time

I think I am afraid of women

Dead Still

soundless keystrokes tapped
out on screen
calling out to someone who
is not here
where
then
outside the realm inside the helm
my boat rides the current
shoreline waves mark my passage
water watcher wake maker

having had these last few years
sober
makes me see what I hid from so long
this is really who I am
the days I fish
the days I write
there is not a lot else
plodding after paychecks
sleeping praying taking out the garbage

everyday life worries me
all day life overwhelms me
I tie up a new salmon rig
set the range on the sonar
check the drag on the reel
click the keyboard
for this day
the other day
the days to come

Maps

pinpoint telemetry
without tubes, rays or screens
compass of the mind
having been here so many times before

where on the globe
precisely are we
at any given time

the mental picture
of my truck
crossing Ocheico Street
same time as yesterday
on my way to work

terrain orientation
one landmark at a time
if only while dreaming
all the other traffic
goes by

Ocean Run Trout

all the bushes
bare
trees leafless
winter
wind, chops up the river top

migrating steelhead
brave chilly current rockbottom
searching for spawn pebbles
creeks and streams
of birthplaces

silversided streaks of
fins splash tailouts
at the stonewall
cast after cast
drift eggs

count the moments
now
until the hour of death
amen

Words and Birds

walked away from writing
to fill the bird feeders
so much comfort in that small action
they call to me

cheep cheep peep peep they call
to me
titmouse hen wren chickadee
sparrows crows jays the yellow thrush
all the backyard birds
make this day
worth the other days

working
wondering
having faith
with hope
and company

Go

plunge ahead
full speed
into this new year

suffer from poor impulse control
along with my other maladies
distracted by
money
women
fast cars
danger
death
bills
backward baseball hats
baggy pants
social unrest
bad breath
magnetic interaction
leaks
squeaks
rattles
mechanical abnormality

all this notwithstanding
plunge on
master the language
create verbal uproar
wake up the dead
pray for the sleeping
this new year

Bio Log

remembering me
after all
Whitman said this is the song of my self

so many nights
at the window alone
watching
waiting
for the words to come
in the fading darkness
almost pale dawn
one or two poems after the whole night
spent watching
waiting
for the words to come

the pages of calendars
fall like leaves in autumns
bail time jail time
in and out of rehab
watching
waiting
for the words to come

now
so much older
with a better view
a cleaner window
watching
waiting
for the words to come

Absolute Delight

there is comfort
in the familiar
like some great pronouncement
(only in regard to my life)
the sound of impact wrenches
the smell of gear oil
Raybestos brake pads
Friday night movies with the wife

comfort
safety
a measure of peace

the familiar
the not forgotten
cars in and out of the stall
covering my tools
at the end of the day

no great pronouncement
(only my everyday life)
the absolute delight
of a poem well written
alone late at night

Catch of the Day

more than one day
crammed into twelve hours
the one boss yelling at the other boss
me
I am hiding in the stall
under the hood
turning wrenches
their petty argument doesn't concern me

my name comes up
I look over
both red faces, stare back
hey I call
I am a burnout
don't care if you both kill each other
I was looking for a job when I got this one

see, the first boss tells the other boss,
he's got a wise ass attitude
(talking about me)
wiseass I say
that implies I care
to be blunt I don't

they huff and puff
like all bosses do
but I put the cars on the street
they get the big share of the loot
if and when I want to go fishing
I go

let me see one of those necktie wearing bean heads
do a valve job
or change a worn out clutch
labor rules in the garage of fools
me I just laugh put away my tools
let them spit and hiss 'til they drop
they get over it or they don't
me
I got fish to catch

Monday Poem

By the boat ramp, circles of color
Trees leaf color reflected in green water
Gold, yellow, umber
Pass the train bridge, current eddy
Scattered ducks dive gulls fly overhead
The wind is still, warm for November
Tide past half full markin time's passage
Rise eyed toward skyline distant
The river flows the birds sing
Peaceful
Outside anyway, inside
The broken heart asks
The downstream answers
Where the river flows
That's where she goes
Along without me

A Wife's Wisdom

stop the poetry
she says
finish the novel
but
it is all blood
from the same wound
what leaps out of me
in these alone hours

chapters are confusing
paragraph by column
having to use the same voice
page after page
when
these
line break
at will
poems
are so much safer

when I look through all the old notebooks
this is who I am
the words
marching
the time going by
one
page
at
a
time

Midway Blues

winter snow blown wind
on the boardwalk
slate gray sky
taking all the color from the ocean
window watchers wait for sun
the air itself, is frozen

two old winos
huddle next to a barrel fire
smoking hand roll
wearing layers of clothes
plastic bags for overshoes

the jetty rocks tipped with ice
footsteps in hard sand surf line
wash out sea foam tar balls
Coney Island morning
long ago
the air itself is frozen

somewhere inside me
is the little boy
I once was
buzzing banging breaking things
scattered comic book images
words from newly read novels
my father's voice
in the background

the boy I once was
might be the key to who
I am now
if I let him
along the shore line on Coney Island

incoming tide covers the jetty
the boy I once was
leaves the beach
starts home
I remember the stairs
now
I would walk down them
not come back again

free here
now
with the silence of poetry
shielding me
joining me
to
the boy I once was

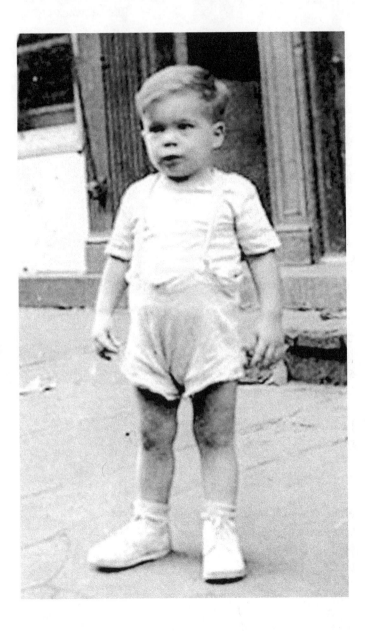

Midway Moves

ALSO BY DOMINIC ALBANESE

Notebook Poems
Bastards Had the Whole Hill Mined
Iconic Whispers
Then-n-Now
Love Is Not Just a Word (with Seb Doubinsky)
Only the River Knows
The Wizard & the Wrench (with Ambika Devi)
Boardwalk Dreams
Disconnected Memories
By Some Happenstance
Poets + Jugglers

Midway Moves

poems by
Dominic Albanese

Poetic Justice Books
Port St. Lucie, Florida

Published by Poetic Justice Books
Port Saint Lucie, Florida
www.poeticjusticebooks.com

ISBN: 978-1-950433-26-1

FIRST EDITION [thus]
10 9 8 7 6 5 4 3 2 1

contents

Midway Moves

after Madison died, o I ran
back to the garage
tool box, bench top, wrenches razor blades
comfort zone

I died inside too
 this fifth decade, so unsure
other friends dead, but the mad dog,
left me gasping
a necktie hands me a repair order
 it is all I can do to keep from killing him
bottle it up, fix the car
  don't let them see the pain

I talk to the cars
whisper to my dead buddies
 I am here
metal, motor oil, bolts, nuts, washers
mindless labor

Madison, my bandit, I mourn you
I have retreated back
to my own private hell, stacking parts on benches
turning wrenches, dying myself a little each day

Chances

take a chance
life is chance anyway
customs habits routines
freeway traffic
sunrise dawn all over

this morning is direct proof
tomorrow came
yesterday left
heaven and earth rolled over again

puffin a grand cru cigar
in the truck on the way to work
humanity lottery one ticket at a time
what ever is in the stall, when I get there
is mine

today will end
job by job, hour by hour
at the next rollover
take a chance
romance
finance
nuts, bolts, washers
death
is no chance at all

Why Anything

why poetry
what
am I after

I seek bodies
attention
with words on paper
emotions
ideas fantasy fiction
personal facts
almost anything goes
the style I choose
    as I write
to no one person
or all who listen

[untitled]

the riverbank, is crowded
baby geese peck weed beds,
adults attend, neck bent in vigilance

the boat passes
back trolling, I whisper good morning
one of the few things keeping me whole these days

Times

like these quiet hours
alone
eight thousand frogs croaked
in the back pond tonight
I could not hear them
without aids
time
has passed
I need glasses to read with
not half the hand speed I once had
but
that is all okay
I have
artificial accompaniment
the night sounds the same
dawn breaks the darkness

times
quiet like this
alone
I am so glad to be alive

Them

o I wonder
where all
my old lovers are
cross country
or dead

the sound
stocking feet
up the stairs
resurrection of one affair
from the ashes of another
blind eyed not hearing the whisper
at the end
this too is part of my wondering
who I am
who they were
here and gone
now and later
hold
my breath
my heartbeat
a pulse at a time
I wonder
this winter's day
the year almost over

Mr. Charley

morning
the mood
as awake
as awake can be
some part of me
stayed in bed
remembering dreams
where the work
was easy
the women easier still

reaching back
to sleepy time
the fish are biting
the sun is shining
there is not a cloud in the sky
dreamy time
just have another cup of coffee
and go to work

morning
the mood
another day
sold by the hour
to the man
his name and face change
but
he is always the same

Holiday Radio

it sure is not
all duck soup
or smoked salmon

holiday cheer
not with-standing
the world is churning
with rumors of war
again

radio stations
still blare bible thumping
holy rollers
all over Alabama

seems like every
Christmas
we never get the message
the prince of peace
is born
Glorify Him

could that really be the key
seems so
to
me

Patsy's Poem

the voice of my
Father
loud, brash, insistent
calling me home for supper

this part of my memory
never comes in picture
only sound
I was afraid of him
ashamed of him too
always yelling,
I carry that blame
to this day

he is long gone
his big voice booms no more
yet
that part of my memory
keeps my heart closed
I try very hard
not to yell
at my grandsons

Haircut

got a haircut third evening
of this new year
groom, preen, admire my gray hair
in a heap on the floor

there have been so many lost times for me
I have been so afraid of who I am not
it is never clear who I am

in the mirror the face, beneath the hair
stares uncomprehending who belongs in this picture

my eyes are as empty as my identity
changing with the days, or the location
no one really sees who I am at that moment
nor do I

what is it going to take
grounded, centered, somewhat peaceful
holding on to the belief, God is
God was always, I am a part of what He created
when do I find a place to belong, I feel so alone
but the company keeps me lonely, even as I claim,
this is what I want

the truth is, I do not know
I have never known,
as I pass from one face, to another year
in a different garage, alone in my little room
take some idea or another, keep it up with real work
not just busy, when does the next time become
this time

Words

I have read
so many books
my ears hurt

the pages
blur by
words go up
in smoke
the lamp grows dim
the blanket has lumps
the bed is hard

someone in the graveyard
is laughing at me
I just get up
go to work
pretend all this is not real
buy more books
chase ideas out of corners
wonder what it all really means

Courage

these days take so much out of me
slugging my way one car after another
someone else's (used) auctioned off overpriced
poor boy going fast help me down the road

been on both sides of the game
broken floor bay shore stink hole
or the tile-textured wall of Ferrari
dozens of garages in between

made some money
smoked some tires
blew up a few motors
put them back together again
rotten old Ramblers
high line exotic swoosh mobiles

have to be more than half done
grease grime burned gear oil
transmission fluid in my hair
working for a living
doing the best I can

somewhere
cigar smoking guy in a straw hat
is fishing with a cane pole
watching the world go by

I am up to my elbows
broken camshaft, bent valves
toothless gears, chain rails gaskets, brackets
soon as I am done with this here's another
now I got to be wishing
    I was fishing
instead of slinging wrenches
stacking parts on benches
calling the cars every dirty name in the book
is it time to go to bed
yet

Deserted

out at night
again
neon
traffic
shadow
lost little
attraction
ear food
eye action
silence
signal boxes
switching
color
ticka tocka click clack
hours pass
echo
more and more

Shore Break

take hundreds of years
to count
all the rocks in the river bottom
took thousands of years
to put them there

glacier ground up mountains
swept away forests
cut crooked pathways
robbed lakes of boulders
louder than any machine
ever invented

later in time
(now)
smooth surface current flow
hides most of the damage
fish see the wreckage
as they swim by
mountains ground to pebbles

as the water
washes time away

Brooklyn Boyhood

say bad
tell you what I'm going to do
you buy three darts, if you don't win
I give the lady a free prize

midway moves
boardwalk dreams
my
Coney Island upbringing
shows sometimes
trying to fast talk my way
out from under
a mess of my own making

slum we called the free prizes
no one ever got the big bears
there was a time when
I wore kangaroo high top shoes
old man's comforts we called them
hair slicked back
selling three darts for a quarter

say bad
tell you what I am going to do
step right up
a winner every time

What Whole Picture

can be crafted
from ashes
of love gone dead
how does the urge to stay
overpower the need
to go

what will I say to
myself
when I wake up
alone

don't treat this like death
it might change
with the seasons

death
    never changes
gone for good
we
    are
        just
            separating
but
    for
        how
            long

Continue to Work on This Issue

I have loved some one
some many ones
they are all a part of me now
whatever I am, some woman gave to me

not my mother
that is another issue itself
the way I laugh
what I laugh at, women taught me
when I am really lost
they at one time or another found me
made the hurt, the sorrow, the loneliness
subside

then this new year
I proclaim
to further work on the big question

3 big questions

who is God
the behavior of fish
the thoughts of women

if
that don't keep me busy
nothing will

Be Right Back

what cause
sets in motion
searching inner rooms
long in need of dusting
childhood prayers
unanswered
repeat soul poems
for wind
women
or being well
a chance
to read my thoughts
as others
confess along side me
life would have no class
without
tears fears rages and confusion